Jesus. The Cross. and Me.

Jesus. The Cross. and Me.

A journey to understand: Who Jesus is. The importance of the Cross. and why He did it all for You and Me.

Stephen Newton

ISBN: 978-0-578-81296-0

CONTENTS

Introduction

This book began as a collection of Sunday morning lessons I taught to my Youth Group in the Spring leading up to Easter 2019.

During that time, I went on a 40-day fast during which I didn't eat meat, sugar, or anything pleasing to one of my cravings. Basically, I ate food that came from the ground. I wanted to get into the mindset of sacrifice to prepare myself for the Easter season. To be honest, I was striving for more in my walk with God, and that required more of an effort on MY part, not God's.

I started with sacrifice: both giving up things I wanted to do and taking up practices to strengthen my relationship with God.

For example, I love movies; all genres of movies, whether it's rom-com (romantic comedy), action, drama, cliffhangers that leave you trying to figure the ending for yourself, if it's a good movie, then that's all that matters.

However, during my 40-day fast, I gave up watching movies, and I took up reading more. I actively set down my cell phone and took time to just sit quietly and meditate on the Lord. I know that's not really a sacrifice for some people, but in the fast-paced world we live in, weeding out distractions and slowing down to do the things that are actually good for us to do can often times be tough for us. Honestly, it was something I felt I needed to do.

My idea for food was simple. Since Jesus sacrificed His fleshly body on the cross for us, I would sacrifice eating any meat. I then embarked on a journey to study Jesus' final days on Earth leading up to the Crucifixion.

The benefits and rewards of fasting led me to a deeper relationship with God. Besides, fasting is Biblical. Jesus taught on the very topic of prayer and fasting, in Matthew chapter 6:5-16. Jesus said "*When you pray…*", *"When you fast…"* it's not "IF you pray" or "IF you fast", it's "WHEN". Basically, Jesus is stating that prayer and fasting are a daily part of the characteristics of the Christian lifestyle.

Weeding out distractions and time wasting activities gave me focus and a sense of purpose. Regular fasting is good for the body and mind, even if you don't do it for spiritual reasons. Fasting, eating better, doing away with time-wasters, and reading more are excellent ways to get a fresh start. But while these actions worked for me, they really helped me realize that I had become comfortable with being comfortable. They also opened my eyes to see others in that same comfortable state.

Seeing the reactions of people or the lack thereof when talking about Jesus or His life concerned me. If we say we believe in the Bible, when it says that Jesus came to die on a cross for our sins and that Jesus came to show us the way to make it to Heaven, then we should be moved by the teachings of Jesus. If our heart is occupied with Jesus, then Jesus should pour forth from our lips and our actions. It should be evident in everything we do. We wouldn't be so quick to reject the moving, the teaching, and the prompting of the word of God. Therefore we would stay on course and keep our hearts aligned with God.

Ultimately, the thesis of this book is the idea that Christians don't have to wait until the Easter season to talk about the Crucifixion sacrifice and Resurrection of Jesus Christ. If we say we truly believe in those supernatural events, then we should celebrate them every day. After all, these are the basis of our belief system, so why does it seem so many Christians only talk about it once a year? And when those events are being discussed, it's like Christians have lost the love, significance, and respect for those events

I believe we as Christians and humanity as a whole need to get back to Jesus. We must understand specifically who He truly is and what it means to have a relationship with Him.

In this book, I pray that when you read it, you hear my heart. I want this book to stir something in you that makes you realize the importance of having a relationship with Jesus for yourself. Maybe this book will help you find your way back to a life with Jesus. Maybe this book will help strengthen and encourage your walk with God. Maybe it allows you to see things differently so you can become a better Christian for this hurting world. I just pray it helps you.

This book won't be a deep theological dive into the life of Christ. Instead, it's about the importance of Jesus in your life, the importance of understanding the Cross, and the importance of understanding why Jesus did it all for you and me.

Since we as Christians should be the ones sharing the Gospel, and since we are supposed to be the hands and feet of Jesus, it's important we truly understand Jesus' reasons for doing what He did. If you believe that

He cared so much about you and me that He willingly laid down His life and died on a cross all for us, you should want to know more about that!

As you read this book, I pray that the love of Jesus flows through these pages and into your heart. I want you to allow the love of Jesus to flow through your actions for your world to see.

Let's take that journey together.

Jesus.

First off, let's set the stakes.

- I believe in Jesus.
- I believe Jesus is God.
- I believe that He was God robed in flesh.
- I believe He came to Earth to be the example to and for us.
- I believe He died on a cross for our sins.
- I believe He died and rose again.
- I believe He did all the things which we read about in the Bible.
- I believe He's coming back for a chosen people.
- I believe in Jesus.

So who is Jesus?

Let's back up.
If I were to ask you to explain who Jesus is, could you?
Maybe some of you could give me a "canned"
explanation of who He is. But do you really, truly know
who He is for yourself?

Even more, if I were to ask you who Jesus is to <u>you</u>, could you give me an honest answer? Do you know who He is? Is He even a part of your life? Or are you not as close to Him as you once were?

You don't have to give me an answer right now. In fact, I just want you to think about these two questions: 1) Who is Jesus? 2) Who is He to me?

If you don't know right now, that's fine. Hopefully, this book will help you discover or rediscover who Jesus is for yourself.

But if you say that you do know who Jesus is, I ask you: "Does your life reflect that to others?"

As I said in the intro, I believe we need to get back to talking about Jesus. And when I say "we", I mean Christians, the church globally. We need to get back to lifting up the name of the Lord through our actions, our worship, the way we treat people, and how we handle things, both personally and socially.

We need to lift up the name of Jesus with the way we speak, how and what we talk about, how we talk to people, who we talk to (without alienating anyone), and by keeping Jesus in our hearts and minds. Because let's face it: if Jesus was really in our hearts and minds our actions would reflect it. It would be what we talk about all the time. The Bible even talks about this. About the mouth speaking of what the heart is full of.

> *"A good man brings good things out of the good stored up in his heart, and an evil man brings evil things out of the evil stored up in his hearts. For the mouth speaks what the heart is full of." (Luke 6:45 NIV)*

I want Christians to talk about Jesus more. I want us to have our focus and attention on God so much that our hearts become full of the things of Him. It must get to the point that He shows through our actions and the words that we speak.

He should be the reason for everything we do. He's the reason I've written this book. I want each of us to have an understanding of who <u>HE</u> is and what <u>HE</u> means to <u>US</u>. Or as Paul told the church in Colossae:

> *"For he has rescued us from the dominion of darkness and brought us into the kingdom of the Son he loves, in whom we have redemption, the forgiveness of sins. the Son is the image of the invisible God, the firstborn over all creation. For in him all things were created: things in heaven and on earth, visible and invisible, whether thrones or powers or rulers or authorities; all things have been created through him and for him. He is before all things, and in him all things hold together. And he is the head of the body, the church; he is the beginning and the firstborn from among the dead, so that in everything he might have the supremacy." (Colossians 1:13-18 NIV)*

✝✝✝

In certain periods of time and through different eras of the church, and the Western culture, people have had a hard time seeing the "humanity" in Jesus Christ. Many of such sentiments can be summarized by thoughts like:

- Jesus is just a god that's hard to please.
- Jesus is just a god that's only tough.
- Christianity is only about morality, do's and do not's.
- God is just a god that's watching over us like a spiritual Orwellian "Big Brother," just waiting for us to mess up so he can hammer us.
- Jesus is only for people who look and act like me.

People somehow forget that Jesus came in flesh, to live among humanity, to show us love in person. So to make Jesus more approachable to popular culture, they tried to make Him "hip and cool". They tried to make Jesus something that was easy to accept, they wanted Him to be *"one of us"* so people wouldn't feel guilty while sitting in a church service listening to a preacher talk about Jesus.

But after too much of that humanity, now it seems more people are having a harder time seeing the divinity in Jesus Christ. By divinity, I mean *"the state or quality of being Divine. Godliness, Holiness, Sanctity."*

Let me explain.

When I was in high school in the early 2000s, there was a popular t-shirt with a picture of Jesus on it looking like *"The Fonz"* from *Happy Days*. Under this "Fonzie-like" Jesus the shirt read, *"Jesus is my homeboy."*

I'm not 100% sure if you can buy that shirt today, but I'm sure you can find something close to it on the internet because that's the way the internet works. But when this shirt first came out, it was everywhere. Every time I saw it, I always had mixed emotions about it.

Yea, that shirt could have meant, "Jesus is so cool, I would take Him everywhere." Or "Jesus is my buddy, my friend. I'd go anywhere with Him. I'd go to parties with Him, roll to the movies with Him. Hey, I wouldn't even be nervous about inviting Him to hang out with my friends." It could have meant all these positive things.

But more times than not, the shirt didn't represent a relationship with Jesus. It didn't mean you would follow Him anywhere He said to go. Instead, it made Jesus just one of the guys, your "Homeboy." It took out all the holiness, the mercy, the grace, the lay-down-your-nets-and-follow-me parts of Jesus. It removed all the things that made Jesus, Jesus. The divinity and sovereignty of Jesus - the things that made people want to follow Him were gone.

Besides, many people have been let down and abandoned by their friends. I myself have had people turn and walk away from our friendship in a vicious way.

And it's that very reason I am glad Jesus isn't my "homeboy." He is my salvation. He is my rock. He is my refuge and strength in times of trouble. He is my example of how I should live my life. He is one that sticks closer than a brother. When people come and go, you can always rely on and put your faith in Jesus. No "Homeboy" will do that like Jesus.

✝✝✝

We need to bring Jesus back to His rightful place in our churches, homes, and lives. We need to give total sovereignty back to HIM and quit trying to do things the way we think they should be done.

Through the generations of time, people in and out of the Church have tried to take away the *awesomeness* that is Jesus. They've even tried to remove the divinity from Jesus' actions so they could become God themselves.

Such "god-like" complexes can be seen in the way they speak, the way they carry themselves, and how they act.

Writers and philosophers have even put pen to paper in order to belittle the works of God, calling people weak for praying to a god, all while considering themselves superior to others because they control their own lives themselves; a.k.a "gods." World leaders have even manipulated people and nations with their words and actions, propping up themselves as "gods" while destroying the lives of their citizens - all for the sake of power.

It's like what *Ian Malcolm* said in the 1993 summer movie classic *"Jurassic Park"*-

"God creates dinosaurs, God destroys dinosaurs. God creates man, man destroys God. Man creates dinosaurs."

I don't think I have to tell you how the rest of that movie goes but, spoilers, when man played God and tried to create, recreate, and control dinosaurs, that creation eventually turned on them and a bunch of people died. It also brought along 2 terrible sequels in that movie franchise, but I digress.

Basically, God created humanity, but humans have ultimately tried to destroy God over time. They have used their thinking, actions, belief in themselves, and lack of belief in God in order to replace God as the ultimate Supreme Being.

Paul Harvey, an ABC radio commentator, put it this way in an April 3, 1965 radio broadcast:

"If I were the devil… I mean, if I were the Prince of Darkness, I would of course, want to engulf the whole earth in darkness…
I would begin with a campaign of whispers. With the wisdom of a serpent, I would whisper to you as I whispered to Eve: Do as you please. Do as you please. To the young, I would whisper, "The Bible is a myth." I would convince them that man created God instead of the other way around. I would confide that what is bad is good, and what is good is square. "

I encourage you to listen to the broadcast clip, or read the transcript in its entirety.

Or as A.W. Tozer once said,
"The Church has surrendered her once lofty concept of God and has substituted for it one so low, so ignoble, as to be utterly unworthy of thinking, worshiping men. This she has done not deliberately, but little by little and without her knowledge; and her very unawareness only makes her situation all the more tragic".
(The Knowledge of the Holy- Preface vii)

I fear Christians have made God so watered down to be palatable to the culture around us that we have removed the deity of Christ. We've made Him our "Homeboy" instead of our salvation, and that is one of the greatest tricks the devil has pulled on us, society, and the world.

We have made God so weak in our lives that it seems that He doesn't even exist everywhere. Could the collective thoughts of people who do not believe in God make others believe that maybe He doesn't exist?

Could it be that, as Nietzsche said, "God Is Dead."

The German Philosopher Friedrich Nietzsche is famous for having penned the declaration that "God is Dead." This phrase first appeared in Nietzsche's *The Gay Science,* a section called *"The Parable of the Madman"* in 1882. However, it was most famously made popular from Nietzsche's work *Thus Spoke Zarathustra.*

Nietzsche stated:

"Whither is God?" "I will tell you. We have killed him—you and I. All of us are his murderers... God is dead. God remains dead. And we have killed him."

Is God dead? Is God still dead? Have wc paid less and less attention to Him where it seems like our lives reflect that statement by Friedrich Nietzsche? Could our actions cause God to be "dead" in our lives, worlds, and society?

As the old adage goes, "If you want a god to go away, just ignore him." The easiest way to kill a god is to simply act like he doesn't exist. So, have we as a people tried to "play God" so much that we think there is no real reason for the "old and outdated" traditions of believing and serving God? And by doing away with them, have we "killed" God? Or to revisit Ian Malcolm, *"God creates dinosaurs, God destroys dinosaurs. God creates man, man destroys God. Man creates dinosaurs."*

Have humanities collective thoughts and actions been the cause or contributing factor to "kill" God?

Let's get back to the topic of Jesus.

Jesus Christ is far beyond what we could ever think up, dream up, or imagine. If you try to understand the mind of God… well, you can't. His greatness, beauty, and splendor are still unknown to many Christians today.

And that's my goal with this book. I want to help us, to help you get to a place where we can know and understand the importance of who Jesus is and why He loves us so much. I want to help the church to have a better relationship with Him so we can be a better example of who He is to those around us.

If we were to seek after Jesus, embrace Jesus, know Jesus for ourselves, and have an honest relationship with Jesus for ourselves, we will have touched the very ONE who is life. In Him resides all truth, values, virtues, gifts, blessings, healings, life, everything! Including your life.

It's why the Bible says:
"In the beginning was the Word, and the Word was with God, and the Word was God.
He was with God in the beginning.
Through him all things were made; without him nothing was made that has been made.
In him was life, and that life was the light on all mankind."
(John 1:1-4 NIV)

When we talk about Christianity, we are talking about Jesus Christ.

Christianity = Jesus Christ.

Nothing more, nothing less. Christianity is not an ideology or a philosophy. Christianity is the "Good News," the beauty, truth, and goodness of existence found in one person. Christianity is Jesus Christ.

What does it mean to be "Christ-like?" It simply means to BE like Christ: To live like Him, to act like Him, and so on. To be like Christ, we take on the actions of Christ, the beliefs of Christ, and the call of Christ.

Our thoughts and actions should reflect the very nature of Jesus Christ.

From the way we deal with circumstances, to how we treat people, to how we approach certain social situations, to how we share the Gospel with believers and non-believers alike, Christ should be visible in our lives.

Think of it this way. If Jesus showed grace, we should show grace. If Jesus was kind, we should be kind. Whatever example Jesus showed in terms of living right to make it to Heaven, then we should be doing that in our own lives. We must be a living example of who Jesus is for others to see.

The Gospel of Matthew mentions one of the first recorded sermons Jesus preached early in His public ministry. We know it as *"The Sermon On The Mount."* This is where Jesus travels into the mountains of Galilee with His disciples and His followers to teach them the way to live.

In plain and simple terms, he showed them how they should act towards others and how they should live their lives on this Earth so they will be blessed in the eyes of the Lord.

That's not a coincidence. Jesus preached and taught about certain things for a certain reason.

Jesus' life and ministry was an example of how we should conduct our lives. It was an example of love, so we could understand how to love others and how our love for Him should be.

Jesus lived what He taught. He showed us how it should be done. That's why it's so important for followers of Jesus to live our lives as an example of Him. If we say we believe in Jesus and His teachings, but we act differently and live our lives differently than what we say, then we are simply no more than hypocrites; merely people pretending or trying to appear to be something or someone we are not. Giving His name a bad reputation, and ultimately giving this hurting world the wrong impression of who Jesus is.

By doing this, we do Jesus a disservice and it will sadly turn more people off of Jesus rather than showing millions around the world who He is. That's not what He wants. Jesus wants us to be the light in this dark world. We should want to show people who Jesus truly is, not the Jesus we have made up in our minds, or the Jesus that fits our lifestyle, or the Jesus that fits a certain political agenda or certain geographical location. Be the Jesus that Jesus came to be.

This world needs Jesus, but we can't show people Jesus unless we have a knowledge of who He is and a relationship with Him for ourselves.

Jesus gave the disciples and those He came into contact with during His ministry a simple invitation: "Follow me." This is the same invitation He gives each of us today. It's up to us to lay down our metaphorical fishing nets and follow Him.

The invitation is there. What are you going to do with it?

It's time to put our attention back on Jesus and focus on the importance of our relationship with Him. Religions, ideologies, philosophies can come and go. They can cause people to be confused about who or what Jesus is. The simple truth is that Jesus came and did away with man's creation of those institutions. He showed us the right way to live, and He taught the importance of a relationship with Him.

As a people, as a church, and as Christians we must get back to realizing how important it is to focus on our relationship with Jesus! If we don't, if we lose that, we stand to lose everything. If we forget or replace our relationship with Jesus, we will ultimately begin to fill those "places" with distractions that will take our attention further and further away from Him.

Some Christians have gotten to a place where they like church but not Jesus. They like the events, the music, the social aspects of church, but they don't want anything to do with the obedience and commandments of Jesus.

Other Christians have gotten to a place where they "like" Jesus but not church. They'll take the blessings and ask for healings, protection, and salvation in His name, but please Jesus, don't ask for too much of my time or money. They have forgotten that those too are His commandments.

When we get to a place where we have a true relationship with Jesus – one where we truly know who He is for ourselves-we will be willing to give Him our all.

Remember? It's all about keeping our focus on Jesus.

One of the ultimate questions Jesus asked in the Bible is:

"Who do <u>You</u> say that I am?"

Before Jesus was crucified, He gathered with His disciples off the coast of Caesarea Philippi. There, He told them of that He must go to Jerusalem to suffer many things, be killed, and that He will rise again three days later. However, before He told them of His death, He asked them one of the most important questions He could've asked: "Who do you say that I am?"

His disciples answered Him by repeating what they'd heard from others. Some said He was John the Baptist. Others said He was Elias (Elijah). Others said He was Jeremias (Jeremiah) or one of the prophets. Some say, some say, some say... Jesus simply replied, "Who do you say that I am"? *(Matthew 16:13-16)*

What Jesus was doing here was showing His disciples that it didn't matter what others said about Him. He knew that some people would spread lies about Him, accuse Him, and spread false information about Him in order to confuse people. What mattered most was that His followers knew who He truly was for themselves.

The same concept applies now. Once we have a relationship with Him and we experience who Jesus truly is for ourselves, it doesn't matter what people say. It doesn't matter if we get made fun of, mocked, or ridiculed for being a Christian. It doesn't matter because we know who Jesus is.

Jesus was once again a living example for us of someone who will be persecuted openly and publically for what they may believe.

The famous British author H.G. Wells, who brought us classics such as *The World Of The Worlds*, *The Invisible Man*, and *The Island Of Doctor Moreau* is also famous for making the acknowledgment of Jesus Christ by saying,

"I am a historian, I am not a believer, but, I must confess as a historian that this penniless preacher from Nazareth is irrevocably the very center of history. Jesus Christ is easily the most dominant figure in history."

Now, if a non-believing historian can and will admit that Jesus Christ of Nazareth is the very center of history, why can't Christians make Him the very center of their lives?

We need to give Jesus His rightful place in our lives; the place of centrality, supremacy, the place where His sovereignty can reign. I wonder what would happen if we gave Him the chance. What would happen if we looked to Him for guidance ALL the time instead of when it's just convenient for us?

I challenge you to put Jesus at the center of your everything. Actually, you should make Him the circumference of your life and fill it up with Him. Our lives should be all about Jesus because Jesus is all about us.

Once you make the decision that your life is all about Him, that's when He takes everything you have and uses it for the Kingdom. He will take everything you have, use it to bless others, and then bless you beyond your wildest dreams.

If you're not sure how or when you'll begin to notice Jesus serving as the driving force of your life, here is a quick and easy test:

Are you talking about Jesus?
Are you thinking about Jesus more?
Do you want to be involved and around the things of God more?
Is your willingness to say "yes" to His will a little bit greater?
Do your actions reflect a Godly lifestyle more than what they use too?

When you make Him the guiding factor of your life, you will make changes in your life and heart that reflect Him. When this happens, you will want to talk about the things of Jesus and ultimately live a life that's pleasing to Him.

When the Bible says, *"out of the abundance of the heart the mouth speaketh,"(Luke 6:45)* that means whatever occupies our heart will be revealed by what we say and do. If you're always talking about negative things, then that's what occupies your heart.

But if your heart is occupied with Jesus, then Jesus will pour out of your mouth and through your actions. It will be evident in everything you do.

✝✝✝

Jesus Christ is God manifested in the flesh. 1 Timothy 3:16 says:

"And without controversy great is the mystery of godliness: God was manifested in the flesh, Justified in the Spirit, Seen by angels, Preached among the Gentiles, Believed on in the world, Received up in glory."
(NKJV)

Jesus in the Bible is the role model to us of who God was and how we should live. Jesus was the living, breathing, moving, functioning image of God; when they saw Jesus, they saw God.

Jesus was known for showing grace and mercy with people, but He was also known for telling it like it was, not sugarcoating it or beating around the bush. If Jesus knew you were doing wrong He would call you out on it, but He would also show you how to correct your mistakes with His teachings and, more importantly, His actions.

Jesus was known for meeting with the criminals of that time. He ate with them, treated them like they were humans, and even used them to further His Gospel. Sitting down to a meal with someone can be a very personal and intimate experience. It's an amazing way to get to know someone and for someone to know and understand you as well. That's what Jesus was trying to show us.

The people Jesus encouraged to follow Him shocked the religious elites of the day. Take Matthew, for instance. As a tax collector in those days, he was basically a criminal.

They would gather taxes for the Roman government, but after they took what was owed to the government, they took a little something for themselves; they did this to make sure the common people would respect and fear them. So in the time of Jesus, Matthew was a thief, and a jerk, and I'm sure people just didn't like him.

But Jesus went up to Matthews's tax collector booth and said, "Follow me." Jesus restored Matthew and made him one of His trusted disciples. So if we were to live to be Christ like, we should strive to live like Jesus, even if it means spending time with people outside our circle who might not be acceptable in a so-called polite society.

However, Jesus is love. Jesus is grace. Jesus is a teacher. Jesus is a friend. Jesus is an example. Jesus is God robed in flesh. And God is everything!

Think about this:
- If Jesus loved evil people, then God loved evil people.
- If Jesus was a friend to sinners, then God was a friend to sinners.
- If Jesus shows grace and mercy to people, then God shows grace and mercy to people.
- If Jesus saves, then God saves. Because Jesus is God and God is Jesus.

John 10:30 says, "I and my Father are one."

God knows all and sees all, so no one sees our sins more clearly than Jesus, yet no one loves us more deeply than Jesus. No sin is greater than the blood of Jesus Christ. No sin is so great that the blood of Jesus can't cover it. We have got to understand that sin is simply not a problem to Jesus. He conquered sin on the cross!

Jesus conquered sin to show us how much He loves us. So if Jesus has already taken care of this for us, then we don't have to live in guilt and shame of our sin anymore. Jesus made a way available for us to live alive and free.

1 Peter 3:18 says *"For Christ also suffered once for sins, the just and the unjust, that He might bring us to God, being put to death in the flesh but made alive by the Spirit."*

LIVE FREE, MY BROTHERS AND SISTERS! LIVE FREE!

1 John 4:8 says, "He who does not love does not know God, for God is love."

Jesus didn't just come to show us a way; He came to show us THE way. He took on sin, the cross, death, and the grave, AND WON! You may be wondering why I love Jesus so much. Because, as the Bible says, "He first loved me."
1 John 4:19 says, "We love Him because He first loved us."

You and I are both able to love Him because He has already given us His love. We are now able to know that love and are able to give that love back because He has first loved us. The very reason we are able to feel and understand love today is because He has already given us His love.

Think about that. Before we could ever sin; before we even knew we were going to sin, God still loved us. He loved us enough to robe Himself in flesh, live among us, show us how to live, and die on a cross for our sins.

Before we could ever love Him back, He gave His love to us.

That's love.

LOVE

The Beatles had it right, and they didn't even know it.
Jesus died on a cross just to show it.

In 1967, The Beatles released a song titled "All You Need Is Love/Love Is all You Need". This was during the height of the "Hippie Movement." The world was at a cultural crossroads, as anti-war and "free love" sentiments had made their way into pop culture. All over our national landscape, you could see signs with written slogans on them, like the now-famous *"Make Love, Not War"*, to protest the Vietnam War.

It seemed like everyone was at odds with each other. Someone needed to stand up and tell people to love one another, to put your differences aside, and just treat each other as human beings. Love. Love. Love.

This song seemed to be designed to help the world think about Love rather than Hate. John Lennon, the formidable writer of the song, even described it as propaganda, saying *"I'm a revolutionary artist. My art is dedicated to change."* Say what you will about The Beatles or John Lennon himself, whether you like their music or not, you can't deny the fact that they changed the course of music and pop culture.

You might be surprised to read that I believe we should take the advice of The Beatles and John Lennon from this iconic song. Everyone could stand to love more in their own lives. Love more, hate less. Be friendlier and less hurtful. If we were to look at the song from a Biblical stance, it makes even more sense, and, in my opinion, has even greater importance for our society.

The Beatles say, "All you need is love", and the Bible in *1 John 4:8* says *"He who does not love does not know God, for God is love."(NKJV)* If the Bible says that God is love, and *The Beatles* say that all you need is love, then you can plainly say that all you need is God, because God is love and God is all you'll ever need!

We are called to love one another. We are called to show others the love of God. How are people supposed to come to the understanding of what God's love is about unless someone shows them that love? You can be God's love to someone. You can help someone come to know what the love of God is truly about by showing them God's love through your actions.

✝✝✝

Does God really love us despite our past and our sin? Are we really worth saving? Does God really care about us? Does God truly love us?

People have asked these questions for centuries, and they will continue to ask them in the future. But they can be answered in one verse.

"But God demonstrates his own love for us in this: While we were still sinners, Christ died for us." (Romans 5:8 –NIV)

So yes, God really loves you despite what you may think or what you may have done.

One of the most important things you can do for yourself, your walk with God, and helping others come to know Him, is to remember and never forget this statement: Before we could ever love God back, He gave His love to us!

That's Love!

My wife and I noticed a common reaction when I originally taught the ideas of this book as a series to my youth group in 2019 leading up to Easter. Whenever we talked about "love" and the "love of Jesus," it seemed to either turn people off or stopped them in their tracks.

Let me back up. Do you remember when I said, that if people were supposed to come to an understanding of what God's love is, we as Christians need to be the ones showing them? Well, in living out that example, my wife and I began to pray that God would use us more mightily in our Church. We prayed our example would be helpful to our youth group and to those that we came into contact with both in and out of the four walls of our church on a daily basis. Basically, we prayed that, when people saw us, they saw God and His love.

We began with one small but impactful act. Whenever we left somewhere, we would say, "Have a Blessed Day." That's it. We began saying it to anyone and everyone we came into contact with, whether a restaurant, gas station, grocery store, the drive-thru, anywhere. We noticed that the majority of the time people would stop in their tracks or give a double-take at us. We could honestly see that person thinking, "Hmm, someone actually cares enough about me or my life." We made it a point to also smile and make eye contact when speaking to anyone. Not a hard or difficult thing to do either.

The same thing would happen when we would ask them how their day was going. We would just talk to them about their day. We actually cared about them, and not just a socially obligated greeting. You know what I'm talking about. We treated people like they are normal human beings.

The sad thing is that people were actually surprised at us asking and starting conversations with them. We live in such a fast-paced society, one that seems to encourage people to only think about themselves. People tend to be caught off-guard by having another human being ask them how their day is going, or by saying "Have a Blessed Day." That, my friend, needs to change, and I think us God-loving, God-showing Christians need to be the leaders in that change.

My wife and I wanted people to know there is a God who loves and cares for them over everything. So why would I put up walls around myself when I go out in public and not take the opportunity to showcase the love of God? Why do so many Christians do that in public? If we have the love of Jesus in our hearts, the Good News of the Gospel, we should want to share it. I want people to know about HIM.

Like I said earlier, while teaching this initial series to my youth group, I was actually shocked by how young people responded to me when I talked about the love of Jesus Christ. This shock even applied to young people who have been raised in the church, and not just young people who didn't know much about Christianity in general. They all acted relatively the same. It seemed this younger generation didn't know that someone actually loved them, or at least they haven't heard it enough to believe it.

Many times, my wife and I would talk on the drive home and we would become sad at how it seemed like these kids just needed to know someone loved them. More importantly, they needed to know that there is a God who truly loves them.

During the series, a young guy in his early 20's started becoming more active in our church by attending our youth activities regularly. One Sunday night at one of our youth services, I talked about the love of Jesus Christ and how Jesus died on the cross for our sins. The service was going great. They responded to the service in a sincerely deep way, and towards the end of the service, they all gathered around the altars of the church to pray.

However, this young guy who has started showing an interest in church stood by himself quietly praying. I felt God tell me to go over to him, hug him, and pray with him. I told him that, there was nothing he had done in his past that could stop God from loving him. Immediately, he broke down and started crying and hugging me back. He didn't say much afterward, so I wasn't sure if the service had gotten through to him, but I had to trust in God and obey.

A week later, we took our youth group to a Youth Convention on Easter weekend, and to put it plainly, GOD MOVED!

The same guy I talked about earlier came, and God moved in his heart and changed the way he lived. On a Friday night at the Youth Convention, the altars were full of young people allowing God to move in their lives. My wife and I prayed for each one of our young people in our group, and I felt God move on me to go pray with the same guy again and in the same way. Remember - trust and obey.

I went over, and we prayed together for a few minutes. I got his attention and made him look me in the eyes. I told him that God loves him. Over and over, I said "God loves you. No matter what your past is, no matter what you have done, God loves you." And with tear-filled eyes, he asked me, "Does God really love me? ME?"

All I could do was say, "YES!" We hugged and prayed some more and God moved in and took over. It was incredible to see God bring understanding to someone and change their life right before my eyes.

I didn't know the whole situation of what this young man was going through. A few days later, he told me he had been struggling with depression and had been feeling all alone. He told me that, when I prayed for him and told him that God loves him, it made him cry, because he never heard that growing up.

Hearing that saddened me so much, but I also know the sad thing is this, his story isn't an isolated one. You never know what someone is going through. You never know who God will place in your path. That's why it's important to show the real love of Jesus to others, not the type of love some Christians think should be shown to others. The type of "love" that is only for the people who look a certain way, or the "love" that is for only certain people whose sin isn't THAT bad.

That's not the love of God. God's love covers ALL sin. God's love is for EVERYONE. It's not up to us to pick and choose who gets it. Jesus died and the cross for every single person in the world.

If we as Christians are indeed supposed to be Christ-like, then we should be the ones showing and giving His love to everyone. We don't get to decide who is "worthy" of God's love or who we think should be allowed to receive God's love. All we're supposed to do is show God's love to everyone no matter the circumstance.
God gives his love freely to everyone, so we should freely show that love to all people, to all walks of life. We have to get to that place in our lives and in our hearts where we realize that, deeply and completely. We must live it out openly in front of people. We should live the love, grace, and acceptance of Jesus Christ so openly that it gets the attention of everyone we meet.

God loves us. We love God.
God loves others. We love others.

There's a hurting world out there, one that needs to know God's love. And you, yes, you, the person reading this book, may just be the one who shows the people in your circle of influence what the true love of God is.

The Cross.

What does the cross represent to you? Or better yet, what does the cross mean to you?

Like I asked before in the "Jesus" chapter, if I were to ask you to explain the Cross, could you? If I were to ask what the cross meant to you, would you be able to give an honest answer?

Maybe some of you could again give me a canned explanation of the Cross. But do you really and truly know the meaning of the Cross and what it represents to you?

Like before, you don't have to give me an answer right now. I just want you to think about it and ask yourself, "What does the Cross mean to me?" "What does the crucifixion mean to me?"

Over the past few decades, it seems that the Cross has lost its meaning with a lot of Christians. Some might think that statement is too far-fetched, that I'm only interested in "shock and awe" or that I don't really know what I'm talking about.

However, my response to those who think my statement is out of line is: "Actions speak louder than words."

I've seen and heard far too many people say that they love what the Cross and the Crucifixion scene stands for, but living out that "meaning" through their actions, isn't believable or possible.

The Cross has become something Christians have taken for granted. It has become a piece of jewelry people wear around their neck while forgetting what the cross represents. It has become a decorative item which people simply place in their homes. Using it as a symbol just to tell other people "Yes, I'm saved." or "I'm a big Christian because I have multiple cross decorations in my home."

I am fully aware that many Christians do like to decorate their homes with crosses or wear a cross necklace around their necks. I'm not talking about that simple and well-meaning act. I'm asking if we honestly understand the true meaning of the cross when we use it as a fashion piece. Have we made it into a symbol with no meaning? Have our efforts to make the Cross a symbol commonly accepted actually caused it to lose its importance?

We must bring the Cross to the place where Christians remember what it truly represents. We must allow its significance to keep us grounded and grateful with our thoughts centered on God.

Honestly, I fear Christians have seen and heard so much about the Cross that they have built up an immunity to it. They have built up a tolerance to the incredible act of love and grace Jesus showed that day while He was hanging on that tree. The cross is a symbol of God's saving grace, and we don't need to dumb down or water down the importance of it simply because we have become "comfortable" with it.

Knowing about it, but not having knowledge of it.

We also don't need to make it something that's cute and fun for a selling point to get people into church. It should be our duty as Christians to present the true significance of Jesus Christ and the Cross to the world.

In the weeks leading up to Easter, my wife and I decided to watch the movie *The Passion of The Christ* with our youth group. Yes, I know it's graphic. Yes, I know it's bloody and gory. Yes, I know it's rated "R." Yes, I know it is extremely rough for some people to watch.

However, before we watched it, I talked with every parent, and told them about the "Jesus. The Cross. and Me" series we were teaching to the youth group leading up to Easter. We received parental consent for every young person, so no need to jump on me about the graphic content of the movie and about my decision to show it to my youth group. But I appreciate your concern.

We wanted to find a way to show our youth group a glimpse of what the Crucifixion scene was like. Words and explanations can paint a pretty good picture, but if the person isn't focused, they can miss out on the details the speaker is communicating. And let's face it, some concepts are better conveyed through visual means.

Having a visual idea of what Jesus went through while He hung on the Cross brought tears to the eyes of our young people. Some who had questions about different aspects of Jesus and the Crucifixion were able to gain an idea of what happened. Although it was a 'Hollywoodized' version, it still was effective and got the point across. They were able to see what we'd been teaching: seeing Jesus go through the amount of torture, pain, humiliation, and death - and going through it all out of love for us.

After the movie, we sat down as a group to talk about certain points of the Cross and Crucifixion. Having an idea in their heads about what Jesus went through opened the minds and hearts of our young people. Some of them may have known some of this, others may have forgotten the story, and others may have forgotten the importance of it. This was a chance to become familiar with it again.

Some people in our youth group didn't know anything about it being as they were starting a new relationship with Jesus. This was their opportunity to experience Jesus willingly laying down His life as the ultimate sacrifice for our sins and for our salvation. Most importantly, it got the youth group talking and asking questions about Jesus. This, in my opinion, was a great thing.

So, let's talk about that scene for a little bit because, if we're honest about it, the crucifixion scene was a brutal display of death and suffering.

It's estimated that Jesus hung on the cross for over six hours. The amount of pain and torture He went through is honestly indescribable. Many writers and researchers have spent many hours studying everything Jesus' body actually went through during the hours He hung on the cross. Scholars have also intently studied the blood that was shed during the crucifixion.

Some have even probably come very close to the exact amount of blood Jesus shed on that day, but honestly, I'm not fixated on the amount of blood He lost while He hung on the cross. I know this; one drop of His blood wiped away all our sins. That's all I need to know. The stripes He took on His back, He took for our healing. The suffering He went through was done out of love for you and me.

Now, I do not mean to diminish the work researchers have done on the crucifixion, and I do not want to discount the amount of torture Jesus went through. It was horrific! The amount of suffering Jesus went through on that day - both leading up to the cross and while He was on the cross - should be studied. It should be talked about and taught.

We have generations coming up in churches who don't even know what Jesus went through during the salvation process of the cross. I bet it's safe to say that the majority of adult Christians in churches now don't honestly and truthfully know for themselves.

Yes, the grace, love, mercy, and salvation of Jesus Christ is accepted by many Christians throughout the world, but it seems like fewer and fewer young people and Christians today have a good understanding of the crucifixion events, and it shows.

Think about it. If young kids aren't being taught about the importance and the meaning of the Cross, then those kids become teenagers who don't know or don't have a strong grasp of the importance and meaning of the Cross. And if it's not being talked about and taught about, those teenagers become adults who may only have a surface level of understanding of the

Cross, but often, it's not a true representation of what the Cross really means.

Remember that one word I mentioned earlier: "Actions".

If we truly believe that Jesus died on a cross for our sins and that it's through Jesus we can have salvation, then our actions would truly show it. It wouldn't be a weekend thing or a Sunday thing. It would be a daily thing.

That's why it's so important that Christians get back to talking about, teaching about, learning about, and focusing on all things Jesus.

Trust me, it'll do us good.

Before Jesus willingly gave up His life on the cross, He was brought - dare I say dragged - from illegal trial to illegal trial. Being led by the Sanhedrin, an elite council of priest elders, Jesus was brought before Pontius Pilate and King Herod (Matthew 27; Luke 23). There, His accusers were focused on finding a way to convict and ultimately eliminate Jesus from their world.

Jesus allowed this to happen. He willingly went through all these events for one reason: YOU.

You need to understand that everything Jesus went through leading up to the Cross and while He was on the Cross was all for you and me. Everything. Think

about that. Everything.
All for You and Me.

Just to name a few.
    Jesus was:
- Beaten.
- Spat upon.
- Mocked.
- Made fun of.
- Humiliated.
- Mistreated.
- Tortured.
- Killed.

ALL FOR US!

Romans 5:20 says, "... But where sin abounded, grace abounded much more."

Jesus died on the cross also to show us grace. He died for our sins. No matter what the sin, He has grace for us all.

Let's pause there.
Did you know His grace is for everyone? There are no limits or restrictions to the grace that Jesus offers us. We just have to accept that grace, use it to turn away from our sins, and then live a life that is pleasing to

God. You need to understand this: no matter what you've done, His grace is for You.

Think about that for a moment. Before you could ever commit a sin, Jesus died on a tree so you could be forgiven of that sin. Before you even knew you were going to sin, or before you even knew you needed to be forgiven of your sins, Jesus took on the beating. He took on the torture. He allowed Himself to be nailed to a cross. He took on the burden and punishment of our sins.
He died upon the cross so that you and I could be forgiven of those sins.

"But God demonstrated his own love for us in this: While we were still sinners, Christ died for us." (Romans 5:8 –NIV)

..."My God, my God, why have you forsaken me?" (Matthew 27:46 NIV)

As the Bible says in 1 Peter:

"He himself bore our sins in his body on the cross, so that we might die to sins and live for righteousness; by his wounds you have been healed." (1 Peter 2:24 NIV)

This means Jesus took our sin upon himself while on the Cross.

During the process of placing our sins upon himself, Jesus cried out to God asking why He was being forsaken. Jesus Christ was fully man while at the same time He was fully God.
The humanity of Christ began to cry out to the divinity of Christ.
In His most desperate time of need, during His time of feeling forgotten and forsaken, Jesus cried out for help.
As Kyle Idleman says in his book *Grace From The Cross*,

"God laid on him the iniquity of us all. The fellowship between God the Father and God the Son was momentarily ruptured. The crushing weight of sin was put on Jesus, and the momentary separation from God is as comparable to the experience of hell itself as you could get."

In that moment, Jesus took on all the sin of the world. He took on all the punishment of sin so we could be given the gift of forgiveness of our own sin. Idelman goes on to say,

"Jesus died our death for sin and he suffered our hell so we would never have to! This is the incredible, incomprehensible high spiritual cost of grace. Jesus was forsaken so we could be forgiven.
At that moment on Calvary, the Bible says that "God made him who had no sin to be sin for us.

Why? That we might become the righteousness of God in him"

"For He made Him who knew no sin to be sin for us, that we might become the righteousness of God in Him." (2 Corinthians 5:21)"

Also, if you haven't read *Grace From The Cross* by Kyle Idleman, I encourage to go pick up a copy for yourself.

So while Jesus was on the cross, not only was He feeling the pain of being tortured and killed, He was also feeling the pain of taking on all of sin and hell for us. Jesus did so all out of love for you and me. He wanted us to have an opportunity to live a life free of sin and free of the torment of hell, if we choose to live that life.

I pray we come back to the place of understanding, love, and respect we should have for the Cross.
Yes, it is a symbol of the act of love and sacrifice Jesus gave us, but I don't want any of us to forget what the Cross truly means.

It was about you and me.
It was THE divine exchange.

Jesus took on our sins so we could be sinless. Jesus took

on Death and Hell so we could be given the opportunity to not ever have to experience them ourselves.

Never forget this fundamental truth. Don't ever get to a place where you doubt that Jesus loves you.

Remember:
Jesus was forsaken so you could be forgiven.
The cross was for Me. The cross was for You!

and Me.

So how do we fit into all of this? How do we fit into the life of Jesus and the Cross?

Like we began the previous chapters, if I were to ask you to explain how you fit into all of this, could you? If I were to ask you about the meaning of Jesus, why He went through all that He did, would you be able to give an honest answer?

I'm sure some of you could again give me a canned explanation of why or how you fit into this. Or I'm sure by now you may have a better chance to work on a more substantial answer. But do you really, truly know the meaning of why for yourself?

Again, like before, you don't have to answer me right now. I just want you to ask yourself, "Why did Jesus do all of this?"

Plainly put, we fit into all of this because Jesus did it all for us. Everything He did was to show us just how much He loves us, up to and including dying on a cross for our sins. He did it for our salvation. He did it to show us the way to heaven so we can spend eternity with Him.

While Jesus was being crucified and then ultimately died on the cross, He knew He was God and He knew all power in the universe was His to command. Yet, He allowed Himself to be mocked, misused, falsely accused, dragged from illegal trial to illegal trial, beaten, spat upon, crucified, and killed. He could have called down angels to stop the Roman guards. He could have said a single word and, in an instant, He could have stopped everything and punished them for their actions.

Yet, out of love for you and me, He allowed it to continue so we could live a life with Him.

In a previous chapter, I talked about how my fear that Christians think they have seen and heard everything about Jesus, the Cross, and the resurrection. They have built up an immunity to the incredible act of love and grace Jesus showed that day while He hung on that tree. I talked about how Christians have built up a tolerance for the Crucifixion and have totally forgotten the importance of why He truly did all those great and marvelous things.

That's why I feel it is so important for us to bring Jesus back to His rightful place in our lives. But without understanding it, it's sometimes hard for us to realize that we are a part of it all. We forget that He died for us.

I believe we need to get the wonder of God back into our lives.

You may ask what I mean by "wonder." I'm talking about the admiration we feel towards God. I'm talking about the inexplicable beauty that is God. I'm talking about a hunger and desire to know Him more, a sense of curiosity about who He is. We need to get wonder back into our lives and into our thoughts.

Time and time again, Jesus shows us the way:
- How to be and live Christ-like.
- How to treat others.
- How to live with humility.
- How to live according to His Mercy and Grace.

Before Jesus was nailed to the cross, He humbled Himself, by getting down own on His hands and knees to wash the feet of His disciples. He showed us the truest form of Christ-like behavior.

Let's be honest, Jesus could've have said, "Listen guys, I'm about to go through a lot. I'm about to be beaten and tortured. I'm going to allow some people to kill me. Do you think you could wash and rub My feet before I have to start this whole torture ordeal?"

He was God robed in flesh, for crying out loud. Yet, He still took the time to show His disciples how much they mattered to Him. It was a way for Jesus to show them how much He loved and cared about them.

God loves us so much that sometimes it's hard for us to understand it. He loves us so much that we can't even wrap our minds around it.

There have probably been times where you thought, "There's no way God loves me." Maybe it's because of your past. Maybe you may have thought He can't love you because you may have doubted He was even real, or that He wasn't all that big of a deal. Believe me: He still loves you.

No matter what you've done or what you've thought about Him, it's still not enough for Jesus to stop loving you. Remember that!

You may ask, "Why me?" Well, let's talk about that.

The Bible says in 1 Peter 2:9-10
9: "But you are a chosen generation, a royal priesthood, a holy nation, His own special people, that you may proclaim the praises of Him who called you out of darkness and into His marvelous light."
10: "who once were not a people but are now the people of God, who had not obtained mercy but now have obtained mercy." (NKJV)

For whatever reason, God chose us. He chose you. The Bible says, *"His own special people"*. We were once a people that would never know mercy. But because God saw it necessary to come down to Earth, live among us, and die on a cross, we have been shown mercy. Because of Him, we can now obtain mercy. We are the people of God.

For a moment, let's focus on the first six words of verse 9: *"But you are a chosen generation"*. You need to understand that. God chose YOU!

Nothing else matters. No matter what the devil may try to put in your way to stop you, God chose you. No matter what people may have said about you, God chose you. No matter what's in your past, no matter what you may be currently doing, no matter what type of doubts you may have about yourself, no matter what, God chose YOU!!

Galatians 2:20 says,
"I have been crucified with Christ; it is no longer I who live, but Christ lives in me; and the life which I now live in the flesh I live by faith in the Son of God, who loved me and gave Himself for me."

God loves you, and He chose you. When you think too much about your sins and your past, it often can make you believe that you can't receive the love that God has for you. You begin to believe you are separated from the love of God. But I want to remind you what the Bible says: nothing can separate us from the love of God.

Romans 8:39 "nor any other created thing, shall be able to separate us from the love of God..."

Jesus loves you. Don't ever forget it. He died on the Cross to show you how much He loves you. Don't ever think that you can do something that could cause Jesus to stop loving you. When you begin to think about your relationship with Jesus in that way, you are actually putting a limit on His abilities and power.

God knows all and sees all. No one sees our sins more clearly than Jesus, yet no one loves us more deeply than Jesus. No sin is greater than the blood of Jesus Christ. No sin is so great that the blood of Jesus can't cover it.

You need to know this. Sin is simply not a problem to Jesus. He conquered sin on the cross! He did it to show us how much he loves us. He conquered death and the grave so we can find the way to Him and spend eternity in Heaven with Him.

"O death, where is thy sting? O grave, where is thy victory?
The sting of death is sin; and the strength of sin is the law.
But thanks be to God, which giveth us the victory through our Lord Jesus Christ."
(1 Corinthians 15:55-57)

✝✝✝

Have you been living for God for years? Are you young in your walk with God? Are you thinking about starting a relationship with God? No matter who you are or where you are, keep going. Find a church community and stay involved. Because when it comes to your walk with God, you must finish what you start.

You can't start off as an adult and end up as a baby, and you can't start off your walk with God already knowing everything. You're not Benjamin Button. You weren't born an old man or woman. You have to give yourself time to grow, develop, and mature in your spiritual life, just like you give yourself time to grow, develop, and mature in your physical life.

Do you want to grow and strengthen your relationship with Jesus? Start with these activities:
- Focus on your relationship with Jesus.
- Follow the teachings of Jesus.
- Stay involved.
- Study.
- Read your Bible.
- Pray.
- Go to church.
- Follow the example of Jesus.
- Find someone who values the importance of a relationship with Jesus and connect with them.

To be honest, not everything will be perfect. No one is perfect. Therefore, we have to trust the process of God's Will for our lives. We must put our faith and trust in the hands of the One who is perfect. And His name is Jesus.

The enemy's goal is division. He wants to divide you from your church, small groups, family, and friends. He wants to separate you from the direction and correction of the Lord. If he can get you or even make you feel like you are divided, like you are all alone on your own, like you are separated and isolated, you will not grow.

That's why we have to constantly stay connected and involved with God and the things of God.

Jesus came to show us the way. Jesus was the living, breathing, moving, functioning image of God. When people saw Jesus, they saw God in action. So, when Jesus dwells in you, people see Him when they see you. Let people see Jesus through your actions.

The more space you make for Him in your life, the more clearly the world, your friends, and your family will see Him.
That is true Christ-like living.

Give Him more room in your life. In fact, give Jesus all the room in your life. Give Him all of you: your heart, thoughts, actions, efforts, and time. Everything you have to offer, give it to God. Give it to Him so He can be seen again through you. The world must be able to see Him through your actions.

It all comes down to this:

God loves us so much that He came down, took on a fleshly body, showed us the way to live, took an awful horrific beating, and willingly gave His life on a tree all so that we could have a better life.

John 10:10 says, and this is Jesus speaking:
"The thief does not come except to steal, and to kill, and to destroy. I have come that they may have life, and that they may have it more abundantly."

He did it all because He loves you. And He'll continue to love you forever.

That's why I'm not ashamed of this gospel. I'm not ashamed to say that I'm a follower of Jesus. He loved me before I decided to follow Him. And he loves you the same.

That's why I encourage you to experience love, hope, peace, and grace. I encourage you to experience Jesus.

I encourage you to discover your relationship with Him today.

✤✤✤

As this book comes to a close, I couldn't let the moment pass without one last encouragement to follow Christ.
- If you are not a Christian.
- If you are not as dedicated to following Jesus as you once were.
- Maybe your relationship with Jesus isn't as strong as it once was.

I encourage you to take the step of faith to become a Christian.

I encourage you to take the steps necessary to get back to your relationship with Him.

Maybe you are already a Christian and you picked up this book to help strengthen your faith. I encourage you to continue taking those steps.

Whether you are a non-believer or a Christian, I encourage you to find a Bible-believing, Jesus-teaching church near you and pour yourself into it. If you've received this book as a gift, I encourage you to talk to that person about it. Talk to them about what you read and how it made you feel.

If you've read this book and you know someone who it may help, give them a copy as a gift and pray over it. Maybe it will be a tool to help them begin their faith journey, renew their faith, or strengthen their faith.

We don't have to stop discussing this topic just because we are at the end of this book. It can and should continue in our lives daily.

Following after Jesus, understanding who He is, seeing how we fit into His plan, and realizing His plan for our lives doesn't end just because this book ends. It's a daily journey. It's a daily process. I encourage you to continue your journey to a fuller life with God.

You must continue to seek out more of what God has in store for your life. Deepen your walk with God. Chase after God. Be the example Jesus Christ laid out for us to follow.

I hope and pray this book has encouraged you. I pray it reminds you of the love and grace of Jesus Christ. I pray it reminds you to show others and give others the same love, grace, acceptance, and forgiveness that has been graciously shown and given to you.

Show someone Jesus through your actions.

Stephen Newton is the Youth Pastor & College and Career/Young Adult Pastor at New Life Praise Center in Seabrook, Texas. He has a heart for people and a passion for the Kingdom of God.
Stephen and his wife, Kaylee, work together in ministry at their local church as well as lead worship and do whatever they can to share Jesus with others.

Connect With Stephen!

Facebook: Stephenhnewton
Instagram: @_stephen_newton
Twitter: @stephen_newton